# Andrew's Art

Set II

WRITTEN BY KASSI GILMOUR

1

Andrew loves to create artwork. His mum says he grew up with a crayon in one hand and paper in the other.

He sees details that others do not. Shadows, light, lines and swirls are all captured in his art book. Andrew drew things fast, and like no one else.

One morning, as Andrew was chewing on his toast, he asked his mum, "What should I compose today?"

Andrew's mum was brewing tea, and she proposed that he create some artwork about the Wild West.

Andrew loved the Wild West and could not wait to get started. He threw down his crust and flew out of the room as fast as a jet.

He drew old streets with
Western vibes.

Wild horses rose up on their
hind feet.

He drew an impressive tree that held many old secrets. Its long branches blew in the wind.

Andrew drew people who could have lived in his landscapes.

A rugged man arriving home after a long, dusty day on horseback.

A hardy lady in a wide-brimmed hat with dark, curly locks.

His work was fine and detailed,
showing long, dusty roads,
old, wooden houses
and grand halls.

He drew

and drew

and drew.

11

At last, Andrew had completed a gallery of Wild West artworks that he was absolutely proud of.

Andrew and his mum invited a crew of artists over. They displayed his amazing artwork for everyone to admire.

# Questions:

1. When did Andrew begin drawing?

2. What details does Andrew see that others do not?

3. Why does Andrew's mum suggest drawing Wild West pictures?

4. What does he draw?

5. What style of drawing do you enjoy?

# How to Make a Sheriff

Begin with the hat, then make part of an oval beneath it.

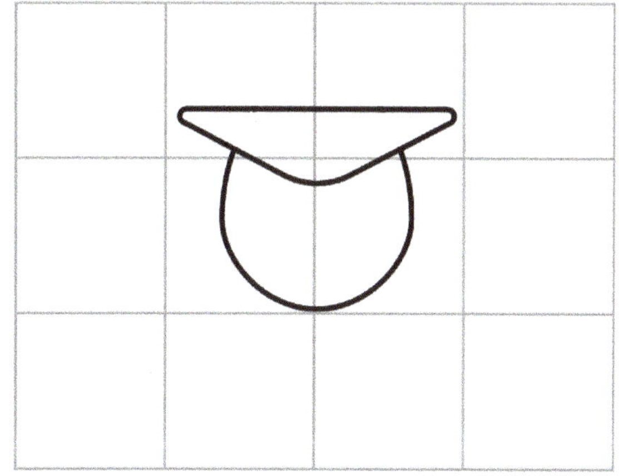

Add a top to the hat. Make the sheriff smile.

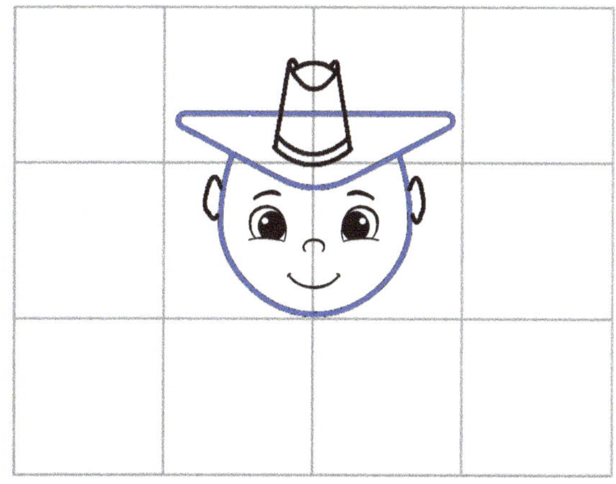

 Give your sheriff a neck and body.

 Add details.

 Lastly, give the sheriff a star.

Who can you show your sheriff to?

# Long Vowels

The grapheme 'ew' represents the long vowel phoneme /o͞o/, as in drew.
This picture helps you remember the sound.